T0077876

THE OTHER SIDE OF MY FACE

SYDNEY PAIGE LAZARE

Order this book online at www.trafford.com
or email orders@trafford.com

Most Trafford titles are also available at major online book retailers.

Print information available on the last page.

ISBN: 978-1-6987-0498-2 (sc)
ISBN: 978-1-6987-0499-9 (hc)
ISBN: 978-1-6987-0500-2 (e)

Library of Congress Control Number: 2020924707

Trafford rev. 12/17/2020

 www.trafford.com
North America & international
toll-free: 844-688-6899 (USA & Canada)
fax: 812 355 4082

To every single person I've known forever, known for a second, met briefly, shared a smile with, shared tears with, and everyone in between. Whatever their impact, collectively they inspired something within me to write.

Prologue

Some people grapple with the complexities that mold
your mind
It's just that those people aren't deserving to know the
beauty inside
It's not your fault they are too blind to see the open door
You can't convince them there are levels beyond the
ground floor

SIDE NOTE:

Don't judge because you don't understand
You got something to say
Write it in the sand

WRITTEN IN THE SAND

To confine me in a shelter you built
Is putting me behind bars handcuffed by your guilt
You tell me I'm too young to take a chance
When the 20 years you got on me are intimidated by my
stance

While you're writing a list of things I can't do
Do me a favor and write them in the sand
Write in the sand so as I prove them untrue
You can watch your words get stolen by the force
underneath you

To have a brain in this day and age
Earns you a spot isolated in society's cage
To want peace without seeing the struggle of war
Is speaking out with nothing to speak for

While you're writing a list of things I can't do
Do me a favor and write them in the sand
Write them in the sand so they can leave without the
trace
Of the ignorance that's stained on your face

I know your toe is sore
Listing what you abhor
But nothing compares to the shame
Of your passion's dying flame
The gift I'll bestow on you
Is a world changed by what you chose not to do
Next time you step in the voting booth
Realize that you voted for me: a voice in the chorus of
the youth

The other side Explained

People make judgments based on what they see, or what they choose to see. They do not always see the emotions that are behind the human, behind the facade; in other words, the other side of the face.

THE OTHER SIDE OF MY FACE

The other side of my face doesn't align with the front
you see
Doesn't align with your assumptions and beliefs
Fails to align with your idea of who I am meant to be

The other side of my face
Is the side you cannot trace
The side you can't assume
The side without a costume

The other side of your face is the side that dictates all
you do
The side that raised you as a soldier and the side that
needs the extra breath to keep pushing through

The other side cannot be defined
The other side is what you take with you and what you
leave behind

#1

In trying to get others to love us, we forget that the love we need most is the love we give to ourselves.

#2

If the world isn't changing, change the world

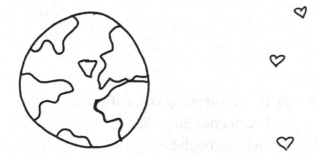

GREEN

She's blocked out the sun
Untouched by the rays
Told that yellow was an evil shade
She stood there
With society in the rain

A raging fire surrounding coals of green
Green cries green lies
Forced through her teeth

Little hands big stance no change
Belittled by
Big hands big stance no chance
Drowning in their crimes

Her heart swims up to breathe
Relief is overwhelming
Hard to welcome in the freshest air
when it's been too far from her reach

Please don't make her play in your pool of green
Splashing around out of your own greed
You can berate her in attempt to destroy her with your
screams
But you can't touch her if she's safe on the sandbar
above your pool of green

She's blocked out the blues
Refusing to submerge herself in your venomous hues
She moves one step at a time
Moving off your spiral staircase and up a straight line

Show her your anger, your fury, your fight
She'll shove the tainted cloud slightly to the right
And allow the sun to scorch your skin
The writhing pain is exposing everything that should
have been
Everything that is
And everything you refuse to see
Cause this flood of envy has left you stained in green

11:11

We can turn back the clock
But we can't relive the time
It may say 11:11
But the world knows 12:39

Can I shuffle my feelings like cards
Again and again until the luck of the draw is in my favor
All the blessed ones think it's hard
While the others can't define a savior

Swiping my smallest finger through a flame
To feed the warmth
To defuse my given name

Adjacent to the crying flame
Wax cascading down my finger
Freezing as it approaches the clock so tame

To be held in my mother's arms
An infant without a hole carved by love
To sleep breathing tranquility not threatened by alarms
Crying with the reveal of the face under the mask of the dove

I can play with time
But I can't play to win
I can dream of a life
Content with all of my kin

I'm dancing with the shadows in my room
Too big to dance on dad's feet now
Too old for guidance, they assume

I talk back and forth between the voice in my head and the beat of my heart
They exchange conversation and empathize the same
They want to dissect the time and rip it apart

Until it's 11:11 and they can breathe strength into the
same wish
"How was your day my love?"
Home feels like home
The feeling was rich

#3

I wonder what would happen if we answered honestly to the superficial question of "How are you?"

The Alarm Clock That Scares

Wake up!
Open your goddamn
eyes!
Wake up!
Open your goddamn
mind!

You can't close your eyes and escape reality
You can't turn your shoulder and preserve "normality"

The alarm clock that scares
Is ignored by the people that brought it to life
The alarm clock that scares
It's us that gave it life

Yes you...the one in denial
Your silence is piercing
Normal's facade is dying

The alarm clock that scares, is scared as well
We have to wake up
And fight like hell

MUSEUM OF US

Close your eyes
Make sure your eyelashes intertwine
Imagine like you did when you were just a kid
It's time to go seek, although you found it more fun
when you hid

Release a glass wall with your mind
Separate you from mankind
Now that you are facing the world in which you live
Is there something you wish you could give?

Look at the museum of us
Look at the destruction made in just that
school bus
Are you happy seeing that child
Losing their pride, losing that smile?

Don't forget that kid in the back
Pulling at her pigtails having a heart attack
That she might make it to school
But a shaking finger might pull the trigger that kindles a
fire with freezing fuel
Do you wish you could enforce a rule?

Look at the museum of us
Watch our people as we cuss
We swear to rid of the pain
Of the loneliness that comes from being so vain

How do you feel about that mom
Blocking out her kids to enjoy her sitcom
Or that anxious dad
Frantically flipping through fairy tales to tell an ending
that isn't so bad
Does any of this make you glad?

Are you delighted by the museum of us thus far?
Now stare into the sea until your little eye spies the
sandbar
Does this view inspire you to write a hit song on your
guitar?

What if I told you the sandbar was a pile of trash
Does this scare you enough to find comfort by ripping
into your stash?
Do you want to go back and pick up the waste left over
from your six-pack?

Look at the museum of us
Look at Mother Nature giving her all
While the world slowly receives the wake up call
You see those children on the street
Raising pictures they painted of the world sweating off
some heat
Is your mind grabbing at a sign to help restore a world
complete?

Look at the museum of us
One last time to see my disgust
I see your quivering lip
Licking the tear rolling off your nose tip

Now open your eyes
Wide enough so yours can meet mine
I think you share my remorse
Change we must enforce
Next time you visit the museum
Are you hoping to see that people finally took a stand?

#4

Masks are getting so good to where we can't even tell
they are being worn

GOING HOME

To look in the mirror and not recognize the image before
your eyes
Is a painted picture that's not admired but despised
To know that the only person you know like the back of
your hand
Is as foreign to you as undiscovered land

Step 1 on the journey home is the realization that you got
lost
Step 2 is the commitment to get there at any cost
Step 3 is forgiving yourself and the ghosts you are
housing in your past
Step 4 urges you to surrender to joy at last

These steps will lead you to the admired image of the
person that shares your eyes
For understanding the clouds in your mind allows the
sun in your heart to rise

Dear Teenage Girl,

I wonder what colors I'll see if I can view the world
from your eyes
You hold up so effortlessly
But the effort makes you die
Tell me each mirror you see isn't telling you toxic lies
Cause your silk red face is soaking piercing cries
I hope you see yellow circling your mind
Don't want to see red burning the delicate coals behind
your eyes
God help me if there's green stuck between your teeth
Right now there's no way for me to see underneath
I wonder if you're sitting now, helpless in your room
Cause I feel your heart screaming but no words are
falling through
If a frigid grey tear is approaching towards your lips
Swear to me it's not about the size of your perfect hips

SHIVER IN THE DARK

I isolated myself to shiver in the dark
I planned to break the heat and burn the calories I longed
to eat

I saw the trail of tears before me
Reflecting the somebody who's nobody
I'm that nobody I see

I planned to drown alone
Depriving my bones 'til my body is toned
And I look like that girl I saw on my phone

I weighed all my problems on a scale
Words were crumbling, they were too frail
I thought it best to shiver alone in the dark
Sculpting an hourglass until the world became captivated
by my art

I thought I was shivering alone in the dark
But I heard a whisper
A swallowed sound of a whimper
I opened my eyes pair of eyes
Aware of how humanity is vandalized

The most beautiful people you could fantasize
Were held captive by the broken chorus in which they
agonize

If you think you've seen perfection on your phone
Flip the camera to see perfection is the beauty of your
own

Sparkly and Pink

I don't need you to save me
I need saving from you
I don't want to wear a jacket
But if I don't I can't bare the things you'd do

If I button up I'm a tease
If I don't I'm forced onto my knees
With scars that might look healed because the strength of
a girl is what makes the King's shield

Let me go to work
You can't begin to fathom our struggle day to day
All they see is pink and wonder how they can get laid
If I button all the way up, I'm a bitch

If I loosen up, I'm a suck-up to the rich
I'll wear the collar, but I won't be dragged on a leash
Bored of their banana trying to get hold of my peach

I'm ashamed of my beauty
I'm ashamed of my age
At 16 I should feel safe turning to the next page
Proud of my body
Proud of my skin
Proud of my face
Proud of my race

I went home today
My mind flooded with words, but none I could bring
myself to say
Let me be a woman
Let me be grace
Let me get opportunities for my skills, other than having
a pretty face

Why should I have to cover up my chest
To force you to keep your behavior at its best
I'm done with this lack of respect
Get over yourself
And get a reality check

#5

You grow up the moment you realize you have more growing up to do

WHO ARE WE?

We never fail to categorize
We never fail to judge
Whether it's spoken or unspoken we always hold a
grudge
We never fail to cry
We never fail to deny
We never fail to comment
We never fail to project what's appealing to the eye

Who are we?
I just feel so dumb
What have we become?
When have we lost our imagination?
Where is the heart of our generation?
Why do we cry at the sight of our face?
Feel like our body is worthless and out of place

Who are we?
We need to be able to look in the mirror and see
ourselves eye to eye
See ourselves as more than just the girl who lost that guy

Who are we?
Yes, who am I? And who are you?
A grown-up isn't grown up until they realize they have
some more growing up to do too

People will tell you your worth
Allow you to believe there's no place for you on this
earth
Yes, it is cruel
But there is only one fool
The one who believes it or the one whose remarks have
been defeated

Who are we?
We all look beautiful
Perfection preserved in its prime
But who are we?
Down on the inside?

Vicious cycle

To those who love the broken telephone,

Stop picking up, and stop dialing.
Just put the phone down.
It's a vicious cycle.

Thank you,
Sydney

Razor blade In an apple

Daddy, what was your biggest fear as a kid?
Well sweetheart...what's yours?
I hate spiders, daddy. I hate spiders. They can bite and
crawl and on top of that they can be poisonous.
What if one is in our house? Daddy, what if one is in my
room? Save me Daddy! Hold me Daddy. Tuck me in.
I was 7 years old.

Dad, what was your biggest fear as a kid?
Well, sweetheart...what's yours?
I hate the dark, dad. I hate the dark. Someone told me a
horror story where Bloody Mary will kill you...but only
when it's dark. What if she is under my bed? What if I
forget to keep on a light? Save me dad. Protect me dad.
Stay awake until I'm fast asleep.
I was 10 years old.

Dad, what was your biggest fear as a kid?
Well, sweetheart...what's yours?
Getting bullied, Dad. Getting bullied.
Someone at school today pinched my cheeks. Someone
else told me not to eat.
What if I believe them? What if I lose confidence in
myself? What if I'm lost? Help me Dad. Talk me
through this Dad. Don't let me believe what they say
dad.
I was 12 years old.

Dad, what was your biggest fear as a kid?
Well, sweetheart...what's yours?
I hate social media, dad. I hate social media.
My phone is screaming at me to be a model instead of
becoming a role model.
What if my fake smile becomes real? What If I loathe
the way I feel?
Heal me Dad. Take my phone away Dad. No wait...I
need it back Dad.
I was 14 years old.

Dad, what was your biggest fear as a kid?
Well, sweetheart...what's yours?
I fear people, Dad. I fear people.
People made those towers fall, people make each other
feel so small, people are telling all these lies, people
bleed toxic cries, it is people who keep making fun,
people who carry guns, people who are trying to hide,
people who force others to keep inside, people who
create the muse, people who choose to abuse.
Save me dad. Hold me dad. But don't tell me things are
not this bad.
I am 16 years old.

Dad, what was your biggest fear as a kid?
Well, sweetheart...on Halloween we were told to look
out for the one guy who would put a razor blade in an
apple.

I can simply state that "something must be done," but that statement means nothing without a solution. So instead, I'm going to encourage you to reflect upon your life, your feelings, and your fears and think of what you can do to restore beauty in this world. Getting angry, without a positive idea for progression, doesn't add to the solution, it feeds into the problem.

WE LIE WITH THE SHEEP

She is a white rose
Effortlessly displaying her figure she's exposed
She lies with the sheep
A harmless image that he keeps

If she stared straight into his soul
Would she unravel the wolf and find it shivering cold?
Or would she knit a blanket of wool
Emptying her cup 'til his is full

A voice of her divine
Used as a footstool to help him unwind
A scream that creates steam against the world's glass
wall
Or a scream contained behind the plastic wrapping of a
doll

She is counted as one with the sheep
A pure image we use to fall asleep
If she is exposed to the world beyond the fence
Her impact too powerful to condense

If you stare straight into her soul
You would unravel her wool and find a starving wolf
waiting with a story to be told

You see a girl

You see a girl, I see a woman
You see "too emotional," I see her callused hands tired
of holding the baggage of womanhood
You see a lovely dress, I see her debating whether or not
she should have brought that jacket
I see that you see her as a girl
You don't see that I see her as the one who will take on
the world

You wouldn't mistake a caterpillar for a butterfly
Society wouldn't dare mistake a man for a guy
So look us women right in the eyes
And respect that just like that butterfly
We are destined to soar,
Not just get by

See us as women
It's about damn time

#6

The amount of time I waste thinking about how much time I'm wasting

Dear math,

I am listless and stolid when it comes to math
X stands for anything
I don't want to stand for anything
I want to stand for something
I don't want to spend my days with eyes scrambling to
find what y equals
I want spend my days finding what I equal

P.S.
I don't care if James bought 3,056 watermelons and
can't return them

Yours truly,
Sydney

Dear parents,

I want to walk a road unpaved
To get to know me without any other projected beliefs
I know you are trying to help
But this is my life, and I somehow got pushed out of the
driver's seat.

#7

A group of 7 walks in groups of twos.
That's it.

Just walk away.

You deserve more.

PICNIC

You are cold but too proud to ask for a jacket
The weight of your feelings remind you how your soul is
a basket
Intricately woven by bendable voices
Choosing the same familiar pattern, as it's easier to
pretend there are no more choices

Words coalesce to mimic wicker
Too fragile to fend for something thicker

The picnic has been planned
Basket in your hand
Feeding another
Until you discover
How you journeyed home with weightless cargo to go
Kicking the pebbles until they roll over your hunched
shadow

Anything with the ability to hold
Has the ability to break
Feather like words
Are often the things that carry weight

People will feed off of your weakness
After drinking from their pool of shame
Desperate for company of the insecure
Because drinking alone is not the same

Risk it For The Feeling

You are willing to risk it for the feeling
Waste yourself again
And if you blur your mind, you hope you'll find an
excuse for what was said
You throw it back
take it in to avoid the world breaking into your natural
skin
Slam it down and throw away the memory of a sin
Don't risk it for the feeling
And throw it all away
There are people here who drown in tears watching their
family slip away

WEAR HER GLASSES

Tirelessly jostled herself past the door
to break into the world towards something more
The wood squeezed her waist
Splinters penetrated through the body, escaping with
haste
Refused to drown in the sea of all she abhors

Broken and bruised, but free of hate
The neglected girl, got in the neglected car, neglecting
the town
accepting her fate

Was she foolish or naive?
Too believing?
Or was she deceived?
Or did she just choose the wrong path?
A path that took on the shape of a circle
The circle that brought her back

It is crucial to know that this girl wore glasses
the circle forced her back into the arms of her broken
smile's cursed ashes

She was nudged to lay in the remains
Make snow angels out of her discarded memories of pain

Stomped on her glasses 'til they were one with the sand
She was thinking in a language no one around would
understand
She was thinking in terms of hope
She doesn't want to recognize the place that taught her
what it was like to cope

The place she knew like the back of her hand
Was blurred enough to label foreign land
Not going to live amongst devils in disguise
Don't want to see the angel faces until they humanize

She will sit in the decorative chair
Because she is unable to see the intricate design she once
noticed as she was ripping out her hair
She recalls that 6 years back
She sat there as her dad explained the exceptions to a
marriage's binding pact

She can't bring herself to see all the detail
She holds up like a rock but still coils like a snail
She won't let her eyes be at ease
Until she wanders off the circle and is finally freed
That girl is me

#8

If you knew then what you know now, you wouldn't be
where you are now
The lesson wouldn't have appeared and it wouldn't have
been learned

WHERE I'M GOING NEXT

An incompetent arrow nudging my compass to the left
To be fighting against the current in the sea of distress
It's telling me where I'm going next
One piece left to complete the puzzle, but that piece is
too complex

8:15 the animals wake
The tiger's stripes are strong
But nullified by the pattern of the snake
12 years old
Venom cold
Restore the warmth from my heart, you keep coming
back to take

A mistaken arrow nudging my compass to the left
I'm not at home in the home that has my address
Give me the box of myself with the originality you
suppressed

Mom packed lunch for me today
Sitting with my math teacher to avoid the wrath your
way
Getting my grades up in hopes to get out someday
To the left is not where I'm going next
I'm reaching for the light that holds hands with the right
Sprinting towards the dream that's in my sight

Fate exists
Fate is real
Fate is the power of what you feel

#9

We can't experience what we are destined for all at once
Sometimes we must must look from a distance,
And smile
Knowing it's ours

ALIGN

Shooting stars are always present
It's us who are absent
Sometimes we miss seeing the radiance of their shine
I'm sorry I was too distracted to see that the open door
was mine

Still we nudge our hearts to talk to the sky
We ask for an answer
To a question we are to scared to find

One day it's shine shall exchange conversation with the
glimmer in my eyes
With the glimmer of hope
Not the leftover gloss from my cries

In the right place
At the right time
We'll align
Holding hands with our presence
We are receiving the long awaited sign

Tight Rope

Right foot forward, left arm up
Left foot forward, right arm up
I'm walking on a tightrope
The thinnest piece of thread
I know I'm walking on eggshells
Even when others say it's in my head
And the rope is thinning
with the only connection on my end
And I laugh stretching a smile too thin
It's possible I'm being rerouted from what my life could
have been
Because why do I keep walking and aching with exhaust
When everyone knows I'm walking just to get lost

Right foot backwards, left arm up
Left foot backwards, right arm up
I'm stepping off of this tightrope
The thinnest piece of thread
No longer walking on eggshells
I'm onto better things ahead

#10

Sometimes we don't recognize our own feelings
Until we recognize why we were drawn to another's
feeling

Don't follow in the footsteps of your shadow

Stop trying to unravel my heart
There's only so much to give when I've got nothing to
start
I am living a life with a life that's not lived
And I can't strip of my shadows the way that you did

But
I'll walk over them
Until they follow behind
Instead of leading the way
I'm going to claim what's mine someday

I followed in the footsteps of my shadow
It did me no good
You tried to unravel my heart
Because you knew if I tried I could

#11

Don't want to be a toy in society's dollhouse
On society's time clock
With society's standards

#12

It's so hard doing what makes you happy
When so many people are happy by seeing you unhappy

But always choose to do what makes you happy.
This is your life.
Build it, protect it.

STOP

Stop is now a sign of suggestion instead of a disciplined
boundary
Limitations are pushed by desperation's unwavering
hands as we long to be free
But freedom has a definition defined differently in every
living mind
But loneliness isn't lonely when it is seen by another's
eye

We ask someone "HEY HOW ARE YOU TODAY?"
Do we ignore the broken strain in their voice claiming
"I'M OK"
Or do we smile and ignore the sign
Because we ignore the fact that we feel the same on the
inside

We stomp on our beauty as we believe mockery
tampered with its name
How we always find a mirror to keep us company when
we are filled with shame

"WHY HELLO THERE, YOU LOOK BEAUTIFUL TODAY"
"NO, NO, STOP IT, YOU ARE JUST BEING NICE"
"STOP FOR A MOMENT AND REALIZE YOU DEFINE YOUR OWN
HAPPINESS' PRICE"

If I set out to run towards freedom
Will I have to lay over a few times in hotels
How can I calculate its distance
Or will I know it when I hear the bells
Will I waste my time allowing stop signs to nullify the
urgency of desire
Or do I throw the nuisances in desire's kindled fire

I can't believe my guffaw is nudged out by rage
I'm foolish after learning freedom is guarded behind our
own minds' cage

If you are amongst the lucky ones who found the cage's
key
It's your duty to inspire and enlighten the rest of society

AT WHAT AGE?

At what age do we stop looking for shapes in the clouds?
The same age we are told the volume of our imagination
is too loud?
The same age we are eased out of fantasy?
The same age we are expected to know who we want to
be?

I am trying to trace it all back
To when we were told magic wasn't real
To when we were told it was weak to feel
To when we were told a coincidence
Was the word for magic's synchronous
Effortless flow
At what age was that?
I really long to know

With all that in mind
I will set out to find
The feeling of magic I left behind
somewhere out there
Where I'm embraced by the air
I'll know when I hit home

But I have to start somewhere
I started looking for shapes in the clouds again

#13

I need you to know that you are not only wanted in this
world, but needed in this world
Your unique self is needed to contribute in unique ways
Ways that only you know how

FONT

It is possible to live a life with a life that's not lived
Because you decided to neglect what you felt had
neglected you as a kid
You didn't mean to write off your dreams but you did
It's not too late to rewrite them in
You lost hope in the world but the world is still placing
its hopes in you
If your story doesn't look right, change the font to
something new
Change the font until it's something that captures the
essence of you
Live a life with a life that wants to live it all
Don't let someone play with you as their doll
To find a deeper meaning
Dig deeper until you find what needs healing
Don't change the word
Change the font
Don't change who you are
Evolve from what you're not

To Feel the Rain

Do you have to walk outside to feel the rain?
Or can you empathize with the bare droplets fogging up
the window pane?
My feet are being molded into the ground
Tasting mother's crying sound
A sculpture is set in place
Base contained
But it's face still bleeds the essence of words forever
chained
Imagine a scream running a marathon through the seams
of your heart
The speaking voice is nullified, but the song is renowned
art
Do you have to walk outside to feel the rain?
Or do you know me well enough to identify my pain?
A baby girl can be born to a woman matured
But that woman still needs the embrace of a baby girl to
know she's still yours
Do you have to walk outside to feel the rain?
Or do I have to strip of the skin you wouldn't know to be
thin
To show you I still need you the same

#14

The bravest thing one could do
Is to look another in the eyes
And allow themselves to cry

#15

Something that is so crazy to me is how someone could
make your entire day and they will never know

#16

Sometimes there is only one shoulder to cry on
That shoulder may be your own
Doesn't mean you should saunter alone
It just means there is only one navigator finding the way
home

Homeless but Have 4 Places to Stay

I'm homeless but have 4 places to stay
I refuse every ride to one
I forgot the way to the other one
I've been losing in the home I thought I won
I'm longing for the gate code to the undiscovered one

I carry heavy bags on my shoulders, choosing my stay
But I'm the heavy cargo, every emotion running on
delay
Claustrophobia is hugging me in a wide open field
My only weapon to fight are my stolid eyes to use as a
shield

No transportation to home number one tonight
Making peace with the feelings, I'm feeling that having
that sense of peace is right

I'm homeless but have 3 places to stay
No rides available to one
I forgot the way to the other one
I've been losing in the home I thought I won
I'm longing for the gate code to the undiscovered one

I'm sitting on a bench with a map in my hands
Figuring out what to do, piecing together my plans
I put my hand on the phone, debating the call
6 minutes later and their number now means nothing at
all

No way to find my way to home number two tonight
Losing the feelings I was feeling when I
First stepped into home number two that first summer
night

I'm homeless but have two places to stay
No rides available to one
Stopped trying to find the way to the other one
I've been losing in the home I thought I won
I'm longing for the gate code to the undiscovered one

I took all the money I gambled, plus more
Felt happy to share some, even with the people next door
I sat for a while and poured myself a nice glass of water
But in this home there's no father, in this place I'm no
daughter

I keep losing more of the home I thought I won
Can I relive the feelings I was feeling when I claimed the
glory after the long fight?
It's been a sleepless night

I'm homeless but with one place to stay
No rides available to one
Stopped trying to find the way to the other one
I lost the home I thought I won
But I'm still longing for the gate code to the
undiscovered one

A keypad ensconced on a blacked out fence
No precise vision of the future, the only option is
shaking with suspense
The energy beyond the fence is radiating towards my
heart
I think someone's calling my name, and I like how they
said it, their voice itself is an art

I'll sit outside the fence for a year or even ten
And someday I'll build a home inside there, it's not a
matter of where, it's when.

And then I'll be home.

How can you sleep on a broken dream?

How can you sleep on a broken dream?
Ignorance shouldn't bring you peace
Ignorance holds you on a short slack leash

How can you celebrate the stripes
Valuing the fruit that hasn't gone ripe
Valuing the stars that strangle the moon
Shooting star shot down and hunted by those with the
silver spoon

How can you sleep on a broken dream?
Watch the horror movie while eating ice-cream
Denying doesn't make you strong
Denying just strings you along
While the powerful sing their song

Don't sleep on a broken dream
This nightmare must be fought by all of us on the
American team
Or expect the scream

Don't sleep on a broken dream.

#17

We are claiming what is already ours
By living our lives
We are rejecting what is ours
By living someone else's life

Heart and Eyes

Your heart and your eyes
Radiate the truths you tuck in the blanket of your mind
The little girl longs to be treated with respect
The little boy builds a wall to force out the emotion he
rejects
Your heart and your eyes
Are as hollow as the holes you house inside
The void that fills up quickly
Or the void that shivers sickly
The conversations exchanged between eyes
Remain honest
Remain unique, unlike tried lies

#18

Mistakes don't define you
The biggest mistake is letting them define you

What Happens?

What happens when the people who have shaped you are
causing you to deform?
What happens when you freeze in the only place that
keeps you warm?
What happens when they speak to you and it feels like
you are being stabbed by thorns?
What happens when they tear you apart and all you have
to give has been worn?
What happens when you lose yourself along the way?
What happens when you are no longer accepted where
you have always stayed?
What happens when you feel so shattered and your heart
has been overplayed?
What happens when you feel like this whole mess is
something that you made?

What happens then?

Well, you keep going. It was all a test.

#19

We all just want to BE
But we refuse to because we are afraid
Of how sheep react to a unique identity

LAUNDRY FOR MY BRAIN

The kids got syrup on his Superman t-shirt
The man spilled coffee on his tie
The woman's new white skirt is stained with dirt
Not to worry it's laundry time
A spill might stain for a minute
But a thought could stain for a lifetime
Is there a machine that could rid of the thoughts staining
my mind
Laundry for my brain
Ringing out the saturated conversations my ears obtain
Purify the cold smudge befuddling my head
Leave a stain on humanity that inspires instead

TALK

The silence is all we can hear
White noise housing crickets in our ears
A waveless ocean raises an eye
A world that's silent is a world with a cry
If you talk to the the world only 1 in 6 respond
But that 1 in 6 knows people beyond
Those people beyond, meet people along
And all those people hear your song
Elated hearts and uplifted souls
Pick up shovels and start filling the holes
They memorize your tune
Racing to voice it too
The 1 in 6's 1 in 6, found the 1 in 6 who owns a mega
phone

#20

Don't think of someone as your missing piece
Think of them as the extra piece you didn't know you
needed but you did.

#21

How many movies are you living in your head?
How many song lyrics have you read?
How many times do you find it true...
That the world revolves around you?

#22

Until we become somebody
We are weird
When we are somebody
Our weird is cool
Because it shows that we are human

But we were human all along

Show Up

I wish you could walk through the tears in my heart
to fill the holes and mimic the fullest parts
I might have to force feed you honestly
'Cause before I can turn around you will spit it out and
leave

Watch me as I walk with my head towards the sky
Self-respect is the mentor that taught me how to fly
If you can't respect me for the woman I am
You won't be able to see me for the person I am
The person who I want to be
The person I am becoming

You are willing to walk away from my surface
refusing to see my intricate layers unfold
I'm a mummy who refuses to lay in your tomb of
counterfeit gold
When the wrapping comes off
My story is being told
Through my exposed shivering core
Either show up on time
Or walk out the damn door

#23

I've been called "unique" many times.
It wasn't intended as a compliment, it was intended as a judgment.
But it wasn't until recently that I realized that "unique" captures the essence of all I ever wanted to be.

#24

Those who assume what's on the other side, might never get the opportunity to know the other side

SONGS

WALK SLOW

If you are gonna walk away, walk slow
If you are gonna let me go, just know
I'll be standing on the road
So cold
Watching you find your way back home

I'm not gonna wash my hands too soon
Not gonna erase your fingerprint 'til June
You promised you'd reach out before this fall
When you're on a path with reception to call

Do me a favor and walk slow
Walk slow enough where I can feel you fade
Instead of you just disappearing before my face
Walk slow so you can think of turning back
Though I know you won't
But I still hope

If you are gonna run away, I can't look
I can't cope with the love you took
Know I'm your biggest fan
I'm blushing in the stands
Watching you from the doorway alone

I'm gonna keep up our pictures 'til May
Look at your smile with too much to say
Gonna close my eyes, pretend like I'm with you forever
Slowly releasing the remains of a sealed letter

Do me a favor and walk slow
Walk slow enough where I can feel you fade
Instead of you just disappearing before my face
Walk slow so you can think of turning back
Though I know you won't
But I still hope

You just said my name for the final time
It's replaying beautifully in my mind
But you are walking away
Effortlessly, without a trace
Of my fingerprints on your hands
You're wiping them off on the sides of your pants

Do me a favor and walk slow
Walk slow enough where I can feel you fade
Instead of you just disappearing before my face
Walk slow so you can think of turning back
Though I know you won't
But I still hope

Is it true?

When the music's too loud you can't hear it
But when it starts to come down you can't feel it
There's a song in my soul that wants to get played
But that part of my soul is slipping away

Look into my eyes
I wanna see the strength in your promise
Saying you won't fade away as I walk my way

I never asked for flowers
'Cause that's fair to you
When all I wanna do is shower
All my love onto You

But now I'm asking for an extra petal
'Cause the last one left me feeling blue
He loves me not
Is that true?

I could watch the rain fall slow
Raindrops racing, only down they go
Why do we play games with them
Betting for which one with fall faster
Cause then they will be gone
That was the plan all along

I'm looking at your eyes
I can't tell if you're a soldier or if you're just not struck
by the fear
Of losing me
Integrity
I'm fading away as I walk away
Into the ghost town where I see my love for you

I never asked for flowers
'Cause that's fair to you
When all I wanna do is shower
All my love onto You

But now I'm asking for an extra petal
'Cause the last one left me feeling blue
He loves me not
Is that true?

But now I'm asking for an extra petal
Cause the last one left me feeling blue
He loves me not
Is that true?

He loves me not
I guess that's true

Set Me Free

Come on now, set me free
I'm not in jail, but everyone's there without me
With crimes of the heart
A crime that sets me apart
I wanna be guilty, but my eyes say I'm innocent at heart

Talk to me baby
You don't know me, but maybe
I could be crazy
I could be crazy

Talk to me baby
You don't know me, but maybe
I could be a thief
Could steal your heart if you let me
Please let me, please let me

When will it be my turn
To be freed from the freedom
'Cause I've been sick of the life I live alone

If everyone's in there
This is so unfair
I wasn't born to navigate this world solitaire

Come on now, set me free
I'm not as fragile as I lead on to be, that's what I believe
And I believe it's true
Crimes of the heart
A crime I'll learn part by part
I wanna be guilty but my eyes say I'm innocent at heart

Talk to me baby
You don't know me, but maybe
I could be crazy
I could be crazy

Talk to me baby
You don't know me, but maybe
I could be a thief
Could steal your heart if you let me
Please let me, please let me

When will it be my turn
To be freed from the freedom
'Cause I've been sick of the life I live alone

If everyone's in there
This is so unfair
I wasn't born to navigate this world solitaire
Set me free

Exit strategy

I'm swallowing my pride
Throat is burning
Heart cold and petrified
Breathing up against the glass
To fog up the picture of my past

I'm stuck in a tunnel
And I can't find the light
Don't let me lose my fight
There was once a blazing fire in my eyes
I cross my heart, it used to burn bright

What if I told you I needed saving
What if I told you I need a plan
What if there is no you
In the sense of you and me
And I'm left alone
With no exit strategy

I'm choking on the air
That's thinning as I speak
Mascara stains and summer rains
My knees are sinking weak
I never got the glow of love blushing off my cheeks

I asked you to cry me a river
So I can flow into your sea
Don't let all my memories
Be pure fantasies
There was once a dream in my mind
But I'm hallucinating and blind

What if I told you I needed saving
What if I told you I need a plan
What if there is no you
In the sense of you and me
And I'm left alone
With no exit strategy

MOVING PICTURE

I'm running through the rain
Tasting the sky as it drips down my lips
I gave up in vain
Don't move, I'm gonna make it on the train

Last time you looked at me was dead
But the picture of you is alive in my head
You hated me these past 4 months
Trying to make amends on this ghost hunt

I still got the moving picture of you replaying in my
brain
That one day you dragged me to the beach in May
That beautiful smile that's moving away
That moving picture
Making me move your way
That moving picture
Making me move your way

I'm speaking to your heart 'cause your mind is tearing
you apart
Know I've changed
I'm trying to fix the clock that you're rushing to restart

I'm speaking to your heart
Leave your mind where you are and just get in the car
Because I need to tell you

I still got the moving picture of you replaying in my
brain
That one day you dragged me to the beach in May
That beautiful smile that's moving away
That moving picture
Making me move your way
That moving picture
Making me move your way

If you have the rose I sent you
Knowing you're sentimental
'Cause I know you
Don't rush to become a ghost in my mind
Don't disappear
'Cause it's you I'm about to find

I still got the moving picture of you replaying in my
brain
That one day you dragged me to the beach in May
That beautiful smile that's moving away
That moving picture
Making me move your way

That moving picture
Making me move your way
I got on the train

In her eyes

What would you say if I told you I'm writing to you
Would you drop your new cards
Knowing I'm your queen of hearts
Or would you play for someone new

I'd love to say I love the way you love her ways
And I hate to say I hate the way I hated seeing you with
her today
I think you see what everyone has been seeing in her
eyes
Something you haven't seen in mine

I wanna see what you see in her eyes
I wanna see something of your divine
I need to to know if what you see in her
Is love for sure
Because you never looked in mine
When my love was on your mind
What is in her eyes
In her eyes

I can't tell if you're replaying in my head
'Cause I'm drinking alone at the party that is dead
And I'm debating you
'Cause I said no when yes was too good to be true
But the feeling wasn't something I knew

I'd love to say I love the way you love her ways
And I hate to say I hate the way I hated seeing you with
her today
I think you see what everyone has been seeing in her
eyes
Something you haven't seen in mine

I wanna see what you see in her eyes
I wanna see something of your divine
I need to to know if what you see in her
Is love for sure
Because you never looked in mine
When my love was on your mind
What is in her eyes
In her eyes

She has every guy out on the chase
They're ready to run the race
Ready to run and claim
That look in her eyes
That keeps them insanely sane
That look in her eyes
Loving who's name?

I wanna see what you see in her eyes
I wanna see something of you divine
I need to to know if what you see in her
Is love for sure
Because you never looked in mine
When my love was on your mind
What is in her eyes
In her eyes

But maybe one time you will look in her eyes
And wonder what it would be like to see through mine

The Game

I thought that I have fallen so hard
But I've never been loved, never been left with a scar
If I were to burn, it will be from playing with fire
Love is a dangerous flame, but it might be worth the pain

Look in my eyes and find my soul
It's empty, waiting for your name to hold
Carve your name and scar my heart
Let my tears drain out the essence of a broken last kiss
I've never had the feeling of a love like this

I can't lose when I have nothing to give away
So why does this pain me that I have nothing to give up
at the close of day
If love is a losing game and
I don't have love
Then I have won the game

I thought all my life I'd been painting with color for fun
But I've never seen the brightest shades, never been left
to soak in the sun
I've never been one to kick the rain
Subconsciously, I sway and refrain from the chain

What if one looks into my eyes and finds my soul
If it fills up only with their name to hold
carve their name and scar my heart
Let my tears drain out the essence of a broken last kiss
I've never had the feeling of a love like this

I can't lose when I have nothing to give away
So why does this pain me that I have nothing left to give
up at the close of day
If love is a losing game and
I don't have love
Then I have won the game

If love is a losing game
And I've found love
Somehow I've won the game

MAYBE

Found a black rose at my door tonight
No trace of red
Sleepless in my bed
Getting frostbite after the cold words that were said

Maybe I deserved it
Or maybe you didn't deserve me
Maybe I deserve the kind of love
Free of thorns
Free to be

Hours turn into days too quickly
Months 'til I'll find the one who'll hold me
But maybe maybe maybe baby
Years will bring me you and save me
Lifetime with red roses
maybe

I should be more than enough in your eyes
your muse
the one you choose
The winning prize you would hate to lose

Maybe it's your blue eyes
and maybe they remind me of the sea
Maybe I'm running to the ocean
Free to swim
Free to be

Hours turn into days too quickly
Months 'til I'll find the one who'll hold me
But maybe maybe maybe baby
Years will bring me you and save me
Lifetime with red roses
maybe

You Don't Know The Other Side Of My Face

For
The other side cannot be defined
The other side is what you take with you and what you
leave behind

Printed in the United States
By Bookmasters